What
Are Earth's
Cycles?

Investigating

Plant
Life Cycles

L. J. Amstutz

Lerner Publications • Minneapolis

Content Consultant: Ed Himelblau, Associate Professor of Biological Science, California Polytechnic State University, San Luis Obispo

Lerner Publications Company
A division of Lerner Publishing Group, Inc.
241 First Avenue North
Minneapolis, MN 55401 USA

For reading levels and more information, look up this title at www.lernerbooks.com.

Library of Congress Cataloging-in-Publication Data

Amstutz, Lisa J., author.
    Investigating plant life cycles / by Lisa J. Amstutz.
      pages cm. — (Searchlight books. What are earth's cycles?)
    Includes index.
    ISBN 978-1-4677-8056-8 (lb : alk. paper) — ISBN 978-1-4677-8335-4 (pb : alk. paper) — ISBN 978-1-4677-8336-1 (eb pdf)
      1. Plants—Juvenile literature. 2. Plant life cycles—Juvenile literature. I. Title.
II. Series: Searchlight books. What are earth's cycles?
QK49.A52 2015
581.3—dc23   2014044204

Manufactured in the United States of America
1 – VP – 7/15/15

Contents

Chapter 1

WHAT IS A LIFE CYCLE?

A green sprout pushes up through the soil. A new life cycle has begun.

A plant's life cycle tells the story of its growth. The life cycle starts when the plant sprouts. It ends when the plant starts to reproduce. Then a new cycle begins.

This is a young flowering plant. What are the three other types of plants?

There are four main types of plants. They are flowering plants, cone-bearing plants, ferns, and mosses. Each plant group has a different life cycle.

PINE TREES ARE PART OF THE CONE-BEARING PLANT GROUP.

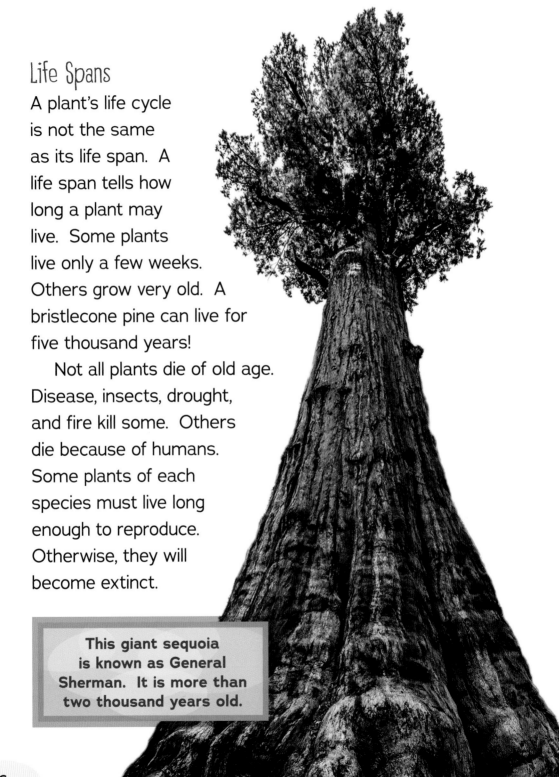

Life Spans

A plant's life cycle is not the same as its life span. A life span tells how long a plant may live. Some plants live only a few weeks. Others grow very old. A bristlecone pine can live for five thousand years!

Not all plants die of old age. Disease, insects, drought, and fire kill some. Others die because of humans. Some plants of each species must live long enough to reproduce. Otherwise, they will become extinct.

This giant sequoia is known as General Sherman. It is more than two thousand years old.

PLANTS DIE WHEN HUMANS HARVEST THEM FOR FOOD OR WOOD. THEY ALSO DIE WHEN HUMANS REMOVE THEM TO MAKE SPACE FOR FARMS OR BUILDINGS.

Chapter 2

FLOWERING PLANTS

Flowering plants make flowers, fruits, and seeds. The plants use these parts to reproduce.

Some plants' seeds are as big as a basketball. Others are as small as a speck of dust. But all seeds do the same job. They protect and feed the tiny plant inside.

The thin shell on the outside of a seed is called a seed coat. Inside are one or two seed leaves and a baby plant, or embryo.

A coco de mer seed can weigh 40 pounds (18 kilograms) or more! What is the seed's job?

See the Cycle

Bean seeds grow in pods *(below)*, much like peas. Soak a bean seed in water for an hour or two. Wait until the seed coat splits open. Pull the two halves of the seed apart. What do you see inside? Can you find the leaves and the root? Where is the food stored?

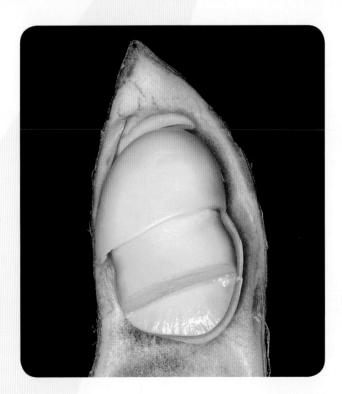

Rice is a seed that is an important food source for many people.

From Seed to Sprout

To germinate, or start growing, seeds need air, water, and warmth. They wait for just the right amount of each. Some seeds can wait for many years. One lotus seed sprouted after twelve hundred years!

When a seed sprouts, its seed coat cracks open. A tiny root pushes down into the soil. A shoot stretches toward the sky. The seedling uses the food that is stored within its seed leaves. In time, it will make its own food. It grows and grows. When the plant is mature, it will make flowers.

Plants can sense gravity. No matter which way the seed is positioned in the soil, the root grows down and the shoot grows up.

All about Flowers

Flowers come in many shapes, sizes, and colors. Some flowers can be the size of a bus tire. Some are smaller than a grain of salt.

Flowers have male and female parts. The male parts are called stamens. They make pollen. Pollen is the sticky, yellow powder at the end of the stamen. Tiny sperm cells are inside each grain of pollen.

The pistil is the female part of a flower. The base of the pistil is called the ovary. It holds the plant's ovules, or eggs. The top of the pistil is sticky to help it catch pollen.

PARTS OF A FLOWER

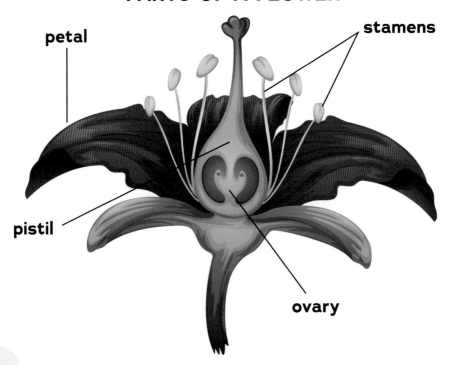

petal

stamens

pistil

ovary

See the Cycle

Find a large, simple flower. Lay it on its side.
Ask an adult to help you slice it open. Can you
find the petals, the stamens, and the pistil?
Remove a stamen. Touch the top of it. Did you
get yellow powder on your finger? This is pollen.
   Next, look at the pistil. Does the top feel
sticky? Slice open the ovary and look inside.
Can you see any ovules?

A hummingbird reaches into a flower and takes a sip of nectar. The bird gets pollen on its beak and carries it to another flower.

How Pollen Gets Around

Flowers cannot move around. So they need help to move their pollen. Some flowers are tiny and have petals that spread wide open. Wind blows their pollen. Other flowers make a sweet liquid called nectar. Insects, birds, and bats drink nectar. When they reach into the flower, pollen sticks to them. Later, the pollen brushes off onto another flower.

When pollen lands on the pistil of another flower, the pollen grain grows a tube. A sperm cell leaves the pollen grain. It travels down the tube into the ovule. Then the ovule becomes a seed.

THE PISTILS OF SOME FLOWERS ARE AS LONG AS YOUR HAND. THAT IS A LONG WAY FOR THE TINY SPERM CELL TO TRAVEL!

From Flower to Fruit

Once a flower is pollinated, its petals fall off. The ovary swells and becomes a fruit. You might think a fruit is something sweet to eat. But to scientists, it is the ovary of a plant and its seeds.

These apples are the swelled ovaries of an apple tree.

Some plants do not need to spread their pollen. In these plants, the pollen stays in the flower and sticks to the pistil of that same flower. The one plant is both the father and the mother of its seeds.

A tomato, a peapod, and a winged maple seed are all fruits. Humans eat some fruits, such as peaches and pumpkins. Animals eat other fruits, such as acorns and thistle seeds.

Dandelion seeds blow away on a windy day.

Moving Day

When a fruit is ripe, its seeds are ready to grow. But first, they must move away. That way, they will not compete with their parents for light, water, and soil.

Wind, water, and animals can move seeds. Dandelion seeds are carried by the wind. Sedge seeds drop into water and float to a new home. Burdock seeds stick to animals' fur.

When the seeds find a good home, they will sprout. Then the life cycle will begin again.

AN ANIMAL EATS A PIECE OF FRUIT. THE SEEDS COME OUT IN THE ANIMAL'S WASTE. THE SEEDS CAN NOW START GROWING IN A NEW PLACE.

Chapter 3

CONE-BEARING PLANTS

Another group of plants makes its seeds in cones. Pine trees belong to this group.

Most cone-bearing plants have male and female cones. The small, papery male cones make pollen.

This tree's male cones are red. What color are its female cones?

The larger female cones have woody scales. Two ovules lie at the base of each scale.

The male cones on a pine tree make millions of grains of pollen. The wind blows this pollen away. It looks like a cloud of yellow dust.

The sequoia is the tallest tree in the world. This huge plant makes its seeds in cones.

A cone's seeds can take a year or more to ripen.

Growing a Seed

When a grain of pollen lands on a female cone, the grain grows a pollen tube. Sperm cells travel down the tube and go into an ovule. The ovule grows into a seed inside the cone.

Spreading the Seed

When the seeds are ripe, they are ready to grow. But first, the cone must open up to free them. Some cones open in hot, dry weather. Others need fire to loosen their scales. Sometimes squirrels or other animals break cones open.

A forest fire can cause some types of cones to loosen their scales and drop seeds. These seeds will have more room to grow because the fire will burn the trees around them.

THIS PINECONE'S SCALES HAVE OPENED.
ITS SEEDS HAVE WINGS THAT WILL BE
CARRIED AWAY BY THE WIND.

When the scales open, the seeds fall out. Some kinds have a wing that helps them drift away. When a seed lands on good soil, it will sprout and grow. In a few years, the new plant will make cones of its own.

See the Cycle

Find a cone from a pine tree or another cone-bearing plant. Squeeze it gently. Is it soft? Did any pollen brush off on your fingers? If so, it is probably a male cone. If the cone is female, look at the scales. Are they hard or soft? Can you see any seeds hiding between them? If so, pull one out and look at it. Does it have a wing?

Chapter 4

SEEDLESS CYCLES

Not all plants start from seeds. Some start from the stems, roots, or leaves of another plant. These new plants are exactly like their parents.

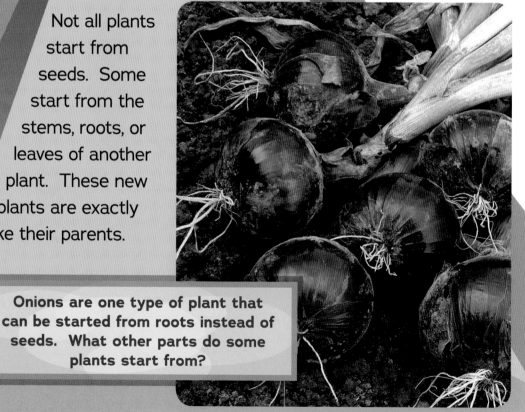

Onions are one type of plant that can be started from roots instead of seeds. What other parts do some plants start from?

Other plants start from spores. Spores are simple cells that can grow into new plants. A spore does not have a seed coat. It does not store food. Ferns and mosses are the two main groups of plants that make spores.

MOST SPORES ARE TOO SMALL TO SEE WITHOUT A MICROSCOPE.

The Ferns

Ferns often grow in shady, damp areas. Some are the size of a dime. Others can grow as tall as an eight-story building.

Ferns grow in two steps. First, they form spores on the back of their leaves. When the spores are ripe, they fall to the ground. They grow into flat, heart-shaped plants. These plants are about the size of your fingernail.

THERE ARE MORE THAN TWELVE
THOUSAND SPECIES OF FERNS.

LIFE CYCLE OF A FERN

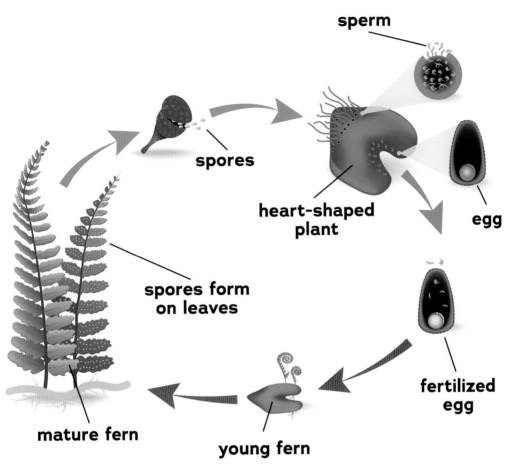

sperm

spores

heart-shaped
plant

egg

spores form
on leaves

fertilized
egg

mature fern

young fern

Next, these small plants make sperm and eggs. The sperm make their way to the eggs. The fertilized eggs grow into new fern plants. Then the cycle begins again.

The Mosses

Moss plants grow closely together like a carpet. They live in damp places. Water is a key part of their life cycle.

LIFE CYCLE OF MOSS

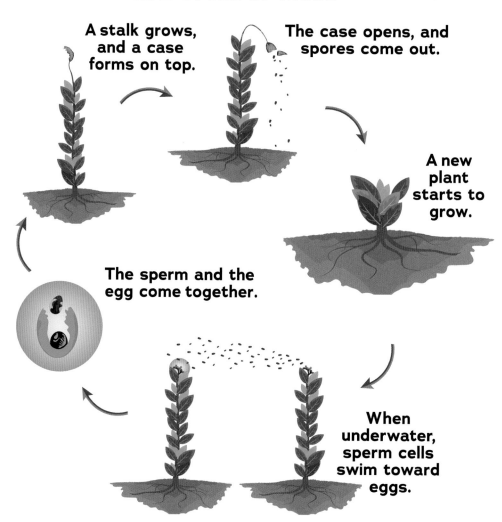

A stalk grows, and a case forms on top.

The case opens, and spores come out.

A new plant starts to grow.

The sperm and the egg come together.

When underwater, sperm cells swim toward eggs.

Each of these stalks contains many spores that will blow away when the pods open.

Moss spores grow in a case on top of a stalk. This case may look like a pod, a vase, or a ball. When the case's lid pops off, the spores blow away. They grow into small plants that look like green threads. These plants make sperm and eggs. A thin layer of water covers these plants. The sperm swim to the eggs. Then the eggs grow into new moss plants.

Other Seedless Cycles

Some plants reproduce without spores or seeds. A few, such as algae, simply split in two. Others start new plants from their roots, stems, or leaves. These plants may make seeds or spores as well. But it is faster and easier to start new plants without them.

For example, a potato is the root of a flowering plant. But each "eye" on a potato can grow into a new plant. Strawberries come from flowering plants too. But strawberries also send out long stems called runners. These runners can put down roots and make new plants.

Tulips are flowering plants. But they usually grow from bulbs, not seeds.

See the Cycle

Find a potato with "eyes," or sprouts, on it. Stick four toothpicks into the middle of the potato, one on each side. Put the potato into a clean glass of water. The toothpicks should rest on the rim. The bottom third of the potato should be underwater. Check the potato each day. Watch for growth from the potato's eyes. Add water as needed, and change it every few days.

Chapter 5

COMPLETING THE CYCLE

Bean plants grow, make seeds, and die all in the same year. They are called annual plants. Many vegetables and grains are annuals.

The life cycle of cabbage takes two years. The first year, the leaves grow. The second year, seeds form. Then the plant dies. This type of plant is called a biennial.

The life cycle of a carrot plant takes two years. What is this type of plant called?

Peach and blueberry plants are perennials. They live and make seeds for many years. Trees and bushes are perennials. So are some smaller plants.

An oak tree is a perennial that can make seeds for hundreds of years.

The End of Life

When a plant dies, it starts to decompose. Worms, insects, fungi, and bacteria break it down. The plant's nutrients slowly return to the soil. They will feed new plants. That way, the cycle of life will go on.

THESE FLOWERS HAVE REACHED THE END OF THEIR LIFE CYCLE.

Science and the Plant Life Cycle

Would you like to watch the plant life cycle up close? Try growing a bean plant on a windowsill. All you need is a clear plastic cup, potting soil, and a few dried beans.

Make a small hole in the bottom of the cup so water can drain out. Add potting soil. Then push three bean seeds into the soil and cover them. Make sure the seeds are near the side of the cup so that you can see them. Water the seeds well. Put the cup in a warm, sunny place and keep the soil moist. Watch your bean plants sprout and grow!

How fast do bean plants grow? To find out, measure your plants every day. Make a chart to record your results. Record anything you notice about your plants or their growing conditions. Note things such as the weather and when the first leaves appear. What did you learn?

Glossary

decompose: to rot or break down

drought: a long period of dry weather

extinct: having died out. A plant is extinct when there are no more living members of its kind.

fertilize: to join the male and female cells to form a new plant

germinate: to sprout and grow into a new plant

life cycle: the series of stages through which a living thing passes from its beginning stage to when it starts to reproduce

life span: the length of time a plant or an animal lives

mature: fully grown or adult

ovary: the part of the pistil that holds the ovules, or eggs

ovule: a female sex cell. The ovule will develop into a seed when it is fertilized.

pistil: the female part of a flower

pollinate: to move pollen from the male parts to the female parts of a flower or a cone

reproduce: to make a new plant

runner: a thin stem that puts down roots to start a new plant

spore: a cell or a group of cells that will grow into a new plant. Ferns and mosses make spores rather than seeds.

stamen: the male part of a flower

Learn More about the Plant Life Cycle

Books

Hirsch, Rebecca. *The Life Cycles of Plants*. Ann Arbor, MI: Cherry Lake, 2012. This book is written from a student's point of view and helps readers understand the life cycles of plants.

Johnson, Rebecca L. *Powerful Plant Cells*. Minneapolis: Millbrook Press, 2008. In this book, students can learn more about cells—the building blocks of plants.

Levine, Shar, and Leslie Johnstone. *Plants: Flowering Plants, Ferns, Mosses, and Other Plants*. New York: Crabtree, 2010. Learn more about how plants fit into the food chain, the climate, and the water cycle with this book on the plant kingdom.

Websites

BBC Bitesize: Plant Life Cycles
http://www.bbc.co.uk/bitesize/ks2/science/living_things/plant_life
_cycles/play
Visit this site to play a game in which you must use your knowledge of the plant cycle to stop a dangerous plant from spreading.

E-Learning for Kids: Plant Life Cycle
http://www.e-learningforkids.org/science/lesson/crab-boat-plant-life
-cycle
Test your knowledge about plant life cycles on this interactive site.

The Life Cycle of Plants
http://www2.bgfl.org/bgfl2/custom/resources_ftp/client_ftp/ks2
/science/plants_pt2/index.htm
This site's interactive activities and animations make learning about plant life cycles fun.

Index

Photo Acknowledgments

The images in this book are used with the permission of: © varuna/Shutterstock Images, p. 4; © Lane V. Erickson/Shutterstock Images, p. 5; © Alexander Petrenko/Shutterstock Images, p. 6; © TFoxFoto/Shutterstock Images, p. 7; © stuttgart0711/iStockphoto, p. 8; © Artography/ Shutterstock Images, p. 9; © Philip Yb/Shutterstock Images, p. 10; © ifong/Shutterstock Images, p. 11; © Blue Ring Media/Shutterstock Images, p. 12; © Spacezerocom/Shutterstock Images, p. 13; © Agustin Esmoris/Shutterstock Images, p. 14; © Vibrant Image Studio/Shutterstock Images, p. 15; © Catalin Petolea/Shutterstock Images, p. 16; © Andreas Zerndl/Shutterstock Images, p. 17; © Jan Bussan/Shutterstock Images, p. 18; © CreativeNature R. Zwerver/Shutterstock Images, p. 19; © Southmind/Shutterstock Images, p. 20; © Felix Lipov/Shutterstock Images, p. 21; © Heiti Paves/ Shutterstock Images, p. 22; © Evgeny Dubinchuk/Shutterstock Images, p. 23; © Photology1971/ Shutterstock Images, p. 24; © Xi Xin Xing/Shutterstock Images, p. 25; © Denis and Yulia Pogostins/ Shutterstock Images, p. 26; © Rob Marmion/Shutterstock Images, p. 27; © Artens/Shutterstock Images, p. 28; © Designua/Shutterstock Images, p. 29; © mapichai/Shutterstock Images, p. 30; © Aleksey Stemmer/Shutterstock Images, p. 31; © Sukpaiboonwat/Shutterstock Images, p. 32; © natashamam/Shutterstock Images, p. 33; © Kesu/Shutterstock Images, p. 34; © Cheryl E. Davis/ Shutterstock Images, p. 35; © Mark Mirror/Shutterstock Images, p. 36; © Kolidzei/Shutterstock Images, p. 37.

Front cover: © iStockphoto.com/Dashinsky

Main body text set in Adrianna Regular 14/20.
Typeface provided by Chank.